# Fun Pony Facts for Kids

Jacquelyn Elnor Johnson

www.CrimsonHillBooks.com

First edition, May 2022.

### Cataloguing in Publication Data

Johnson, Jacquelyn Elnor

Fun Pony Facts for Kids

Description: Crimson Hill Books trade paperback edition | Nova Scotia, Canada

| | |
|---|---|
| **ISBN:** | 978-1-990291-80-7 (Paperback - Ingram) |
| **BISAC:** | JNF003110 Juvenile Nonfiction: Animals - Horses<br>JNF003220 Juvenile Nonfiction: Animals - Animal Welfare<br>JNF054170 Juvenile Nonfiction: Sports & Recreation - Equestrian |
| **THEMA:** | SK - Equestrian & animal sports<br>YNNJ24 - Children's / Teenage general interest: Ponies and horses<br>WNGH - Horses and ponies: general interest |

Record available at https://www.bac-lac.gc.ca/eng/Pages/home.aspx

Book design: Jesse Johnson

Crimson Hill Books
(a division of)
Crimson Hill Products Inc.
Lawrencetown, Nova Scotia
Canada

Crimson Hill
Books

*A beautiful pure white pony.*

*Ponies are gentle and friendly, but they also have some secrets!*

# Do you know ponies?

If you have your own pony, or your biggest wish is to get a pony, you probably already know a lot about them.

They're friendly and intelligent.

They're brave, sweet-natured and gentle.

They are patient.

We also love them because they like people. They're always happy to see their owners.

Though modern ponies live indoors in their stalls and stables, they'd always much rather be outside with their herd, even in cold weather. Their second-most-favourite thing to do is spend time with you, perhaps on a trail ride with other ponies and riders, or in a riding lesson, or competing at a Pony Club or Gymkhana event.

Ponies are the pet you need if you want to learn to ride a horse. They are fun to get to know. Like some other pets, such as dogs and cats, they each have their own distinct personality.

Ponies also have secrets. These are interesting, quirky, and just plan odd fun facts about them. That's what this book is all about.

Once you've read it, you'll know more about the secrets of ponies' lives than most other owners and riders know, even some of the most experienced pony-loving people!

*This herd has ponies and donkeys.*

## A pony is not just a baby horse

Ponies don't grow up to be horses. They're ponies for all of their lives.

A pony is a type of horse. All horses, including ponies, are in the species named *Equus caballus*. They share their family tree.

There are more than 600 registered breeds of modern horses. 200 of these are ponies. They live almost everywhere in the world except the coldest places where there is no grass for them to eat, such as the High Arctic and Antarctica.

There are two basic things to know about ponies.

*Icelandic Pony showing off their spectacular mane.*

Once you know these two things, you will understand almost everything about them.

**1.** Ponies are a prey animal.
**2.** Ponies are a herd animal.

All animals are either predator animals or prey animals. The predators are the hunters. The prey animals are who they hunt.

Wolves, hawks, all types of cats, snakes and humans are all predators.

Even though they are big and strong, horses are prey animals. So are goats, sheep, songbirds, elephants and giraffes. Prey animals only eat plants or plant products, such as seeds.

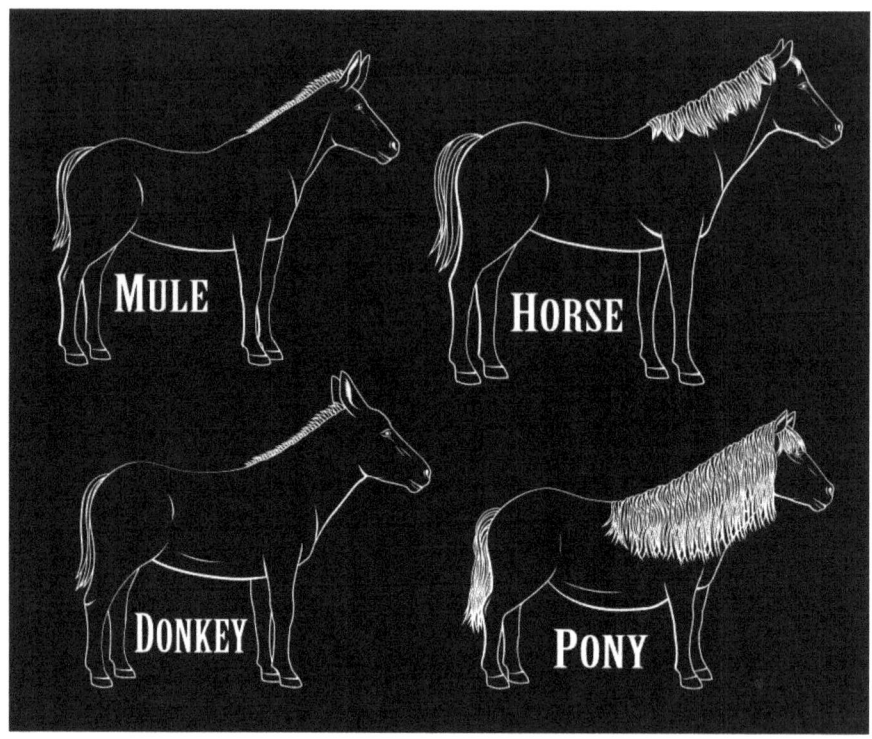

*A pony, compared to animals that are pony cousins.*

Prey animals are always on the look-out for their predators. They're always ready to run or fly away if they can or fight if they have to.

Most prey animals live in family groups because they need each other for protection. A family group of horses or ponies is called a herd. Herds usually have a lead mare. She's called this because she is responsible for leading the herd to food and fresh water. There's also a lead stallion, who is the herd bodyguard, making sure everyone stays safe. Mares along with their babies or youngsters make up the rest of the herd.

Ponies are social. They live in herds for safety and companionship.

# Why aren't ponies just called little horses?

Ponies have a different body shape than horses. Ponies are less sleek and more barrel shaped, with shorter legs. Their manes and tails are thicker and are usually longer. They have a shorter face, with a shorter muzzle. Their ears are a bit smaller than horses' ears and a lot smaller than a donkey's ears.

Ponies also grow up into adults faster than horses do. For their size, ponies are tougher and stronger than horses.

# Pony cousins

Close cousins to ponies are:

- **Donkeys** – Very friendly, they like to be pets.
- **Mules** – This is the animal you get when you breed a female horse with a male donkey.
- **Zebras** – Once there were many types of zebras, but today there are only three. The rest have become extinct. Wild zebras live only in Eastern and Southern Africa.

*Pony Fun Fact:*
*A pony's back legs are longer and stronger than their front legs.*

*Zebras, Rhinos and Tapirs are just some of the species related to ponies.*

More distant cousins, but still related to ponies, are:

- **Rhinoceros, or Rhinos** – a plant eater that lives in parts of Africa and Asia.
- **Tapirs** – Like a wild pig, they live in parts of Central America and South-east Asia.

What do all these pony cousins have in common? The answer is in their toes. They all have an odd number of toes, unlike most mammals, and people, who have an even number of toes. There are only 16 animals in existence today that have an odd number of toes.

# Why did all the horses in North and South America vanish?

Millions of years ago, there were the ancestors of modern horses living in what is now North America. With plenty of open plains lush with grasses, lakes and rain for water and few enemies, they thrived. We know this is true because there are many fossils of Eohippus, the oldest ancestor of horses, in North

*Ancient people painted horses on cave walls in Europe more than 40,000 years ago. Surprisingly, these cave paintings look remarkably like the Mongolian Pony of today. Could it be the horse these ancient people knew is similar to one that's still alive?*

American museums today. Eohippus lived from 56 to 33 million years ago.

Other, larger, horses came after Eohippus. Then, perhaps 8,000 to 12,000 years ago, horses completely vanished from North America. It seems to have happened all at once. Scientists today call this the Quaternary extinction.

No one knows exactly why the Quaternary Extinction happened, or why it didn't happen anywhere else, only in North America. All the horses in Asia, Africa and Europe survived, though there were fewer of them. It might have been climate change, too much competition for food and water, or even that all the horses were killed off, perhaps by humans. Experts have different theories, but no evidence of exactly what happened, or why.

It wouldn't be until explorers from Europe sailed west, with their horses, that horses would return to what is now United States, Mexico, Central America and Canada and all the countries of South America.

Imagine how surprised the native peoples of the Americas must have been when these explorers appeared, mounted on these magical beasts!

# Did ponies arrive in North America centuries before horses did?

We don't know, but it's possible. What we DO know is that the Norsemen and Norsewomen took ponies to Iceland from their homes in what is now Denmark and Norway. They took ponies, instead of horses, because ponies are smaller and eat less than horses. They also took cows, pigs and goats.

Some of these Norse people sailed even further, going all the way to the large island that is now Newfoundland, a part of Canada and the furthest-east point in North America?

They did start farming colonies in Newfoundland 500 years before Christopher Columbus reached North America.

*This Shetland Pony was bred for riding.*

As settlers and farmers, the earliest people to arrive in what is now North America and South America arrived, we think, about 25,000 to as many as 40,000 years ago. They must have come with their animals, but no real proof of this has been found. Why there were horses and ponies in Asia, Europe and Africa for so long, but none in the Americas until only 500 years ago or so remains a mystery.

# Ponies with jobs

Ponies are not an animal that developed on their own in nature. They were bred from horse breeds by people for specific reasons. Usually that reason had to do with a job people needed done.

Some were bred to be small and cute, the pampered pets of wealthy people or royalty.

Others were bred to work for people, carrying their burdens, pulling wagons, as pit ponies pulling carts in coal mines or, more recently, for children and smaller adults to ride.

Today, ponies are no longer forced to work in coal mines. Almost all modern ponies are either feral, or they are kept as pets for recreational riding.

### *Pony Fun Fact:*
*All ponies and horses can turn their ears backwards to hear sounds that are coming from somewhere behind them.*

*This is the Australian Pony. Like almost all pony breeds, it is named for where it was first bred.*

## People and ponies have been friends for a long time

At first, and for a very long time, probably many thousands of years, humans thought that horses were good to eat. That's if they could manage to capture and kill them. Horses were and still are bigger, stronger and faster than any human.

It took people a very long time to realize that maybe they should eat other things and make friends with the horses. As you might imagine, the horses were wary of this plan. They weren't sure humans could be trusted. Eventually, some did begin to work for people, hauling their belongings and letting people get

*Most ponies aren't much bigger than a large dog.*

on their backs, in exchange for food, shelter and protection.

This probably happened at about 6,000 years ago in many places in what is Europe, Africa and Asia and possibly also in North and South America. There were no horses at all until modern times in Australia.

## How big are ponies?

Most creatures and all people are measured in feet and inches, or in metres and centimetres.

Ponies and horses are measured in hands and inches throughout the English-speaking world.

*Most horses are much larger than most ponies.*

A hand is 4 inches (just over 10 cm). It's called a "hand" because it's the same as the width of an average man's hand.

The first number is full hands, then there is a point, and the next number means plus some inches. So, for example, a horse could be 16.2 hh, or hands high. This means they are 16 hands plus 2 inches tall or 66 inches tall or just over 167 cm tall.

Ponies are always 14.2 hands or shorter in Canada, the United States, India, New Zealand or UK, or 14 hands or less if they live in Australia.

Ponies are always measured from the ground to their withers. Withers is the name for the tallest point of their body (not including their head and neck). It is a spot just behind where their neck ends and their back begins.

One other animal you might know is usually measured from the ground to their withers. That animal is the dog. Other large animals, like cows, are usually measured hoof to hip.

# Little horse, BIG pony

Some horses are smaller than some ponies. This is because there are some horse breeds, such as Arabians and Haflingers, that sometimes or usually are smaller than 14 hands tall.

Caspian and Yakutian are two horse breeds that are always shorter than 14 hands.

Even though they're petite, they are called horses because they are true horses. They have the sleeker body shape, longer face and personality of horses, not ponies.

Miniature horses are always smaller than ponies, but they are also true horses.

# How old can ponies get?

Horses are seniors by the time they're in their late teens. Most horses live about 25 to 30 years, although with better food and good care, they can live longer. The oldest-known horse in modern times lived until he was 62!

### Pony Fun Fact:
*Ponies can take short naps standing up.*

*Feral Icelandic ponies run free in Iceland.*

Ponies generally live longer than horses. Ponies normally live until age 35 or 40 and sometimes beyond then. Sugar Puff was a Shetland-Exmoor cross (that means one parent was a Shetland Pony and the other was an Exmoor Pony) who lived to be 56. He taught many children to ride and was such a sweet lad that the family that owned him, in West Sussex, England, sometimes allowed him to come in the house!

**Pony Fun Fact:**
*Ponies can swim, though many of them don't seem to like it.*

# Why there are no wild ponies?

Maybe you've heard about an island conservation area or park you can visit to see wild ponies. They live in herds and enjoy life with no job to do except show up to entertain visitors.

But are they really, truly wild? Probably not. The reason is that all these wild ponies are actually feral ponies. Feral means they – or maybe their parents or grandparents or great-grandparents – were tame, but they escaped or got loose. There are many animals in the world that this is true for. Wild dogs, wild cats, even wild budgies that used to be pets but got loose and now live a wild, or sort-of-wild, life. They're all actually feral animals.

So are the Mustangs of the American West, the Brumbies of Australia, the Chincoteague Ponies of Virginia and Maryland in the U.S. and the Sable Island Ponies of Nova Scotia in Canada.

It's exciting to think that somewhere in the world, in some very remote place, there could still be truly wild ponies running free, but this is fiction, not a fact.

# Have you ever seen an albino pony?

Albino means they have no melanin in their skin or eyes. It is melanin that gives skin, or eyes, their colours. Albinos have pale or white skin and pink eyes.

Being an albino is inherited. This means it's something you get from your parents. If you're born albino, you

*White is a rare colour for ponies. This one is wearing her white winter coat.*

don't grow out of it. It's very rare. Being albino can happen in animals and also in people.

People or animals who are albinos have very sensitive skin and usually have trouble seeing, or they might be blind. Otherwise, they're just as healthy as any other animal or person.

But none of them are ponies. The reason is if a pony is accidentally albino, it won't live long enough to be born.

Some pony breeds can be born white, or near-white, or they might turn white or light gray. None of them have pink or red eyes and they aren't albinos.

Most white ponies actually aren't white, they're gray. Truly white ponies are rare, but you might be lucky enough to see one!

# Pony babies

All pony babies are called foals until they're one year old.

When they're born, their legs are almost as long as they'll be when they're an adult.

Just minutes after they're born, they can stand up and walk. On the same day they'll be outside, running, kicking and playing with the other foals in their herd.

# Baby teeth

Just like human babies, foals are born with no teeth. In only a few days, their first teeth appear and soon, all baby ponies have 24 baby teeth.

When their permanent teeth start to grow in, they lose their baby teeth. This happens when they're about two and a half years old.

By the time your pony is five years old, all her or his baby teeth will be gone. They will have between 38 and 44 adult teeth, depending on their breed.

### *Pony Fun Fact:*
*Horses first evolved about 40 million years ago.*

*This is a feral Exmoor Pony mare and foal in England.*

# PONY terms

**Foal** – any newborn pony.

**Yearling** – any pony who is one year old.

**Colt** – a male pony, from when they're a foal until they're four years old.

**Filly** – a female pony, from when they're a foal until they're four years old.

**Stallion** – a male adult pony.

**Gelding** – a male pony who is not able to get a mare pregnant.

**Mare** – a female adult pony.

**Senior** – a Stallion, Gelding or Mare who is 20 years old, or older and is retired.

*This is an Appaloosa pony. Appaloosa isn't a breed. It's any pony that is spotted, in any pattern. Many pony breeds can have Appaloosa babies.*

## Predator or prey? The eyes have the answer!

You can always tell if an animal is a predator animal or a prey animal by looking at their eyes.

If their eyes are on the sides of their head, they're prey. If their eyes look forward, on a flat face, they are a predator.

The reason is that predators need to look straight ahead, to see the creatures they want to capture. Prey need to be able to look in all directions to spot danger, but usually don't have very good distance vision. They need to spot things that are close and an immediate danger.

# What big eyes you have!

All types of horses, including ponies, have almost the largest eyes of any land animal compared to their body size. Their eyes are bigger than elephants' eyes!

The only creatures with even bigger eyes than ponies and horses are seals, whales and ostriches.

# Looking both ways

With eyes on the sides of their heads, ponies can see things in front of them, beside them and almost all the way behind them. They can't see directly behind their own tail, a rider on their back or under their own nose.

They are able to see two different views at one time – one with each eye. Each eye sends its own message to their brain.

That's completely different than the way human eyes work. Our eyes see two slightly different images, but then our brains combine those two into one image to understand what we are looking at and also how far away it is from us. This helps us focus and also gives us what's called depth perception.

Depth perception is being able to see the width, length and depth of objects.

Horses and ponies are good at focusing on just one thing, but not so good at depth perception. They are better than we are at detecting movement from a distance. They aren't as good as people are at seeing details in things that are close to them.

When you see a pony moving his or her head up and down, it's because they're trying to get both their eyes to give them a better view of something.

## More about pony eyes

Like many animals, ponies have better vision at night than humans do.

They can also see in colour, but not the way you are able to. Most people can see three colours (yellow, blue and red) from which all the other colours are made. This is called trichromatic vision.

Ponies have dichromatic vision. They can only see two colours – blue and yellow, and the combination of those colours, green. They can't tell the difference between red and green.

*Pony Fun Fact:*
*Welsh Ponies were first bred in Wales more than 3,000 years ago.*

*Pony Fun Fact:*
*Ponies are tiny when they're born but their legs are almost as long as they will be when the pony is an adult.*

*This Welsh Pony is showing off some healthy chompers.*

*Ponies have super-sniffer noses and whiskers that aren't just there to decorate their faces!*

## Why ponies have whiskers

When a pony is grazing, their head is close to the ground, where it can be hard for them to see the freshest, most delicious blades of grass.

Their whiskers are really sensors able to feel anything they can't see because it's right under their noses!

Their muzzle whiskers help them find the best food and fresh water and understand their surroundings. It's how they know they are in a familiar and safe place. Their whiskers tell them how close they are to something.

They also have whiskers over their eyes that tell them when something could poke them in the eye!

People who take their horses or ponies to competitions used to trim these whiskers because they thought it made their pony or horse look better. Now that we know the important job whiskers do, it's against the law in some countries and also for most major competitions to cut a pony's or horse's whiskers!

For many years, it has been illegal to cut a horse's or pony's whiskers in Germany and Switzerland. As of 2021, anyone who trims their horses' or ponies' whiskers before any FEI International Federation of Equestrian Sports event (this includes the Olympics!) gets kicked out of the competition!

# 4 toes, or 20?

Almost any horse or pony breeder, trainer or experienced owner will tell you that all horses, including ponies, have only one toe per foot.

Ponies are classified, or grouped together, with other animals that have an odd number of toes, like tapirs, rhinos and zebras.

A horse or pony hoof has just one big toe. That's what just about everyone thought. Then, just recently, some experts said, "wait a minute, maybe that isn't true." They say there are three toes, or maybe four, or possibly five toes per horse or pony foot.

Here's why they're saying this. These experts took a closer look at ancient horses. There was Mesohippus,

*Ponies can have all of the horse coat colours, but most are brown. These three have unusual colours of (left to right) Appaloosa, Chestnut and Black.*

a horse that lived 35 million years ago. Then they took another look at Dinohippus, the horse ancestor who lived 5 million years ago.

What they found is astonishing. It seems that the very earliest creatures that would eventually evolve into horses had five toes per foot. But over time, as horses developed and became larger, they didn't need all their toes.

On modern horses and ponies, it is possible to make out very small bones attached to both sides of each hoof. These are all that's left of what used to be more toes.

Ancient horses had four toes on their front feet and three toes on their back feet.

# What part of your pony is constantly growing?

Here's a big hint – you also have this!

If you said their mane, you'd be partly right. As long as it's groomed, a pony's mane will keep growing. If it isn't groomed, it will stop growing when it's as wide as a pony's or horse's neck.

What other part of their body, and yours, constantly grows for all of their (or your) life? It's their hooves, which are made of keratin, just like fingernails. Keratin is a protein that is also in hair.

Just like human fingernails and toenails, a pony's hooves need to be trimmed. A hoof grows about ¼ to ½ inch (or a bit more than a half centimetre to just over one centimetre) per month.

Hooves grow a bit faster in summer and a bit slower in winter. That's also just like human fingernails.

Trimming hooves is a tricky job, usually done by a specialist called a farrier. You need the farrier to trim your pony's hooves about every four to six weeks.

# Froggy feet!

Every pony has froggy feet. In fact, they've got four of them!

Not only that, a horse's or pony's four frogs are often called their "second heart."

*The fluffy long fur around this pony's ankles is called feathers.*

The frog is the triangle-shaped cover over the cushion in the bottom of their foot. The frog, with this cushion, serves like a shock absorber in a car, evening out all the jolts and bumps of anywhere they walk or run. It helps protect their bones and joints from injury.

The frog, and cushion under it, also pumps blood back up a pony's or horse's leg, towards their heart. The heart loads this blood with oxygen and nutrients and sends it back out to everywhere in the body.

### *Pony Fun Fact:*
*Ponies can take short naps standing up.*

## Big-hearted ponies

The average horse or pony has a much bigger heart, compared to their body size, than a human heart.

Thoroughbred racehorses have hearts that are ten times as big as a healthy adult human heart!

So just how big is your pony's heart? Here's an easy way to find out. It is 1% of their total body weight.

## Some ponies wear shoes

Horseshoes are made of metal and shaped like a U. They protect the pony's hooves.

Over millions of years, horses developed to be strong when they are wild. But modern horses have different lives, spending most of their time in their stalls and paddocks. Unlike their wild ancestors, they don't get enough time to run around and wear down their hooves naturally. Many modern horse breeds have bad feet.

Wild horses were very healthy, running barefoot. That's generally not true for domesticated or tame horses that live with and work for people. Their feet need extra protection to keep them from being injured. Their metal shoes also help their balance and give them more traction on wet, snowy or muddy roads and on hills. Traction means gripping the road, not slipping or getting stuck.

There are many types and sizes of shoes for ponies and horses. They are fitted by an expert called a

*A farrier trims hooves, checks foot health and fits shoes on ponies or horses.*

farrier. He or she is also the one who trims their hooves regularly.

Some owners don't like putting traditional horseshoes on their ponies. Instead, they say, regular hoof care from a farrier and possibly also wearing hoof boots or glue-on shoes are better.

Some ponies are fine without shoes. But if a pony seems to have sore feet, stands oddly, does hard work or is a performance pony in competitions, they need shoes.

### Pony Fun Fact:
*A foal can stand up just minutes after she or he is born.*

# Biting and kicking

You'd probably get in lots of trouble if you decided to kick somebody. Or bite them.

But that's how ponies defend themselves when they feel threatened. They'd usually rather just run away, but when that isn't possible, such as when they're in their stall, they are just fine with a quick bite to whoever is causing them problems. Or a swift kick.

Also, like every animal, they don't know how to apologize!

# How old are you, little pony?

How can you tell a pony's age?

You could look in their records or their passport, if they have one. A faster way is to just look in their mouth.

Look at their teeth! The six front teeth change and wear down as they get older.

# Ponies have super sniffers

Chances are your pony will smell you coming before they see you! That's because their super noses can smell things way better than people!

They use their smelling superpowers to find fresh water and healthy food and to recognize each other.

*Horse laugh – is this pony enjoying a good joke?*

Foals use their sense of smell to find their mothers among the herd. They can do this as soon as they're born. A mare knows the scent of her own foal, even in a large herd with several new babies.

## Can ponies laugh?

It looks like this pony is laughing, but they aren't. Ponies can't laugh. They put their heads up and curl their lips to get a good sniff of the air. This tells them who's nearby.

When they do this, it's called the Flehmen [FLAY-men] response. You will see ponies do this when they come across any unusual or strong odour.

## Ponies can smell if there's medicine hidden in their water, food or treats

Even if they're really hungry, they won't eat if they smell something hidden in their food or treats. And even when they're thirsty, they won't drink if the water, or the bucket it's in, smells different than they're used to.

Their super sense of smell also helps them identify predators, such as bears or wolves.

Ponies can smell fire or approaching storms. Being able to smell danger gives them an early warning system so they can run to safety and shelter.

## Ponies don't like windy weather

Wind makes ponies worried and confused.

Wind moves things around more. Like all horses, ponies are very aware of where they are and everything else that is around them. As prey animals, they are always ready to flee from danger. Things moving suddenly can scare them, because it might mean a hidden enemy, like a wolf, is stalking them.

Wind also carries scents from further away. This means there are more scents to sniff and figure out what they are and if they're a signal of danger. Another reason wind confuses ponies is it carries sounds from further away.

*This Shetland is alert to sounds that are in front of him.*

## Can ponies hear through their teeth and their hooves?

If there was trouble coming, would your teeth, or maybe your feet, let you know?

The answer is "YES!" if you're a pony.

When a storm is building or a volcano is about to erupt, there are vibrations in the ground. These are usually too small for people to notice, but most animals can. Ponies use their hooves to sense these vibrations. And also, incredibly, their teeth.

When they're grazing, their face is just above the ground. It is so close, that they feel the slightest ground movements through their teeth, even when they're munching on grass.

Like many animals, a pony's super senses to spot the signs of danger are much better than any human's.

# Ponies are excellent listeners!

If you were a prey animal, would you rather be really good at seeing your enemies from far away? Or, would you want to be able to hear them from far away?

The choice all horses, including ponies, made is to have vision that is pretty good, but hearing that is exceptional. Many creatures can hear more, or better than people can.

Ponies can hear sounds from much further away than any person can. Do you think you could hear a sound from almost three miles (or 4,400 metres) away? Ponies can!

They can also hear high-pitched sounds that are higher than people can hear. But it also seems that they can't hear some low-pitched sounds that we can hear.

# Pointy ears!

Can you wiggle your ears? Not everyone can. But every pony can move their ears, tilting them and even pointing them in two different directions at the same time.

*This Chestnut Shetland Pony mare is deciding whether to ignore something she's noticed or run.*

They use their ears like super-sized satellites, flicking them in all directions to collect every sound from all around them.

## Should I stay or should I go?

When a pony stands still and raises his or her head, it's because they've heard a strange sound or caught a suspicious smell on the air. If the sound is in front of them, they will point both ears in that direction.

If they're super alert, with their head up, eyes wide, nostrils flared and ears pointed in a direction, they're signaling to all the other horses and ponies around them that it's time to run!

# Tail Tales

Pony tails can tell you what a pony is thinking, but only if you can translate Pony Talk!

Here's what the Tail talk means:

**Holding their tail high over their back** – they're feeling excited or happy to play.

**A tail that is flat against their hind legs** – they are afraid of something or in pain.

**If their tail is pressed tightly between their back legs** – they're nervous about something.

**Swishing their tail wildly**, like a flag in a storm – they are frustrated or angry.

# Ponies are touchy!

Ponies are so sensitive to touch, they can feel it when even one fly lands anywhere on their body. You will see them twitch just the muscle where that fly is to chase it away.

They don't like to be patted. Instead, they'd like some gentle stroking on their neck. Never touch their belly or legs until they know you very well and have learned to trust you. To a pony, those places are just too sensitive for strangers.

*Ponies are very affectionate with their owners.*

# Pony talk and what it means

**Sighing** Ponies sigh for pretty much the same reason people do. It might mean relief, as you take her saddle off after a long ride. Or it might mean they're just bored or don't want to have to do something all over again.

**Blowing** Ponies blow out air suddenly to say, "Hello!" They also do it when they're curious.

**Nicker** Is a soft sound horses and ponies use to greet each other, or people they like.

**Squeal** is what ponies do when they distrust something. The louder the squeal, the more worried your pony is.

**Whinny** is a loud sound that means "Where are you?" to another pony who's lost, or it can be a distress signal to the herd. Neighing is another word for whinnying.

**Snort** is another loud sound and a way that herds communicate to be sure everyone hears. It means fear or danger.

**Clacking** is a noise young ponies make by clicking their teeth. They do it to tell the older members of their herd that they're just little and to please not hurt them. They stop clacking after they're two or three years old.

Tame ponies eat grass or hay, which is dried grasses.
Wild ponies eat  some other plants or tree leaves
when they can't find fresh grass.

# Pony Love

Ponies show their affection for each other, or for people, by nudging them, nuzzling, grooming and touching.

When they like another horse or pony, they will stand together, back to front, swishing their tails gently to keep flies off their friend's face.

They might also gently nip each other, getting at itchy spots the other one can't quite reach.

If they like you, they will let you stroke them gently, making circles with your hand on their head or neck.

If they reach out and blow a gentle puff of air in your face, it means they really like you! They usually only do that with their owners.

# Ponies are snackers!

Ponies spend more time eating than anything else they do when they're awake! As grazing animals, their bodies have developed to be almost constant snackers. When they go two hours or more without food, they will get a stomachache from being hungry.

As plants-only eaters, or herbivores, the main thing they eat is grass. Hay is dried grass. Compared to horses, ponies eat half as much grass or hay, when you compare them by weight. This makes ponies a less expensive pet to have than a horse.

Ponies like things that taste sweet, like apples and carrots. And they like salty tasting things, too. They avoid anything that tastes sour or bitter.

Ponies, like all horses, are very interested in the way their food and water tastes. That's because they have 25,000 taste buds in their mouths. As a human, you have around 9,000 taste buds. That's less than half as many!

## Ponies can't burp. Or throw up.

Something almost all people and mammals can do is burp and vomit to get rid of gas or something bad they swallowed. No horse, including ponies, can do either of these, so everything they swallow has to go all the way to the end!

Not being able to get rid of something bad they ate is why they get stomachaches called colic.

## Do ponies know their own names?

Yes, they can learn their own names and some other words, like commands. It isn't the word, exactly, that they're learning, but more the tone of voice. With a horse or pony, if you want them to learn a word, you have to always say it in exactly the same way for them to understand.

### *Pony Fun Fact:*
*Most ponies live longer than most horses.*

*Shetland Pony mare and foal.*

## Ponies love play fighting!

Have you ever seen ponies or horses out in their field, rearing up, nipping each other's

faces and knees? They'll do this for a few minutes, take a break, and then start up again.

It looks like little kids play-fighting with their brothers or sisters, except they'd get in big trouble if they bite each other!

Ponies and horses don't. It's their idea of having a great time with their friends.

### *Pony Fun Fact:*
*Ponies would always rather run than fight.*

# What type of pony is the strongest?

Shetland Ponies are the strongest breed of ponies, compared by size. They're one mighty-mini of a pony!

They can pull up to four and a half times their own body weight! That's more than almost any horse can do.

Shetland Ponies are named from the place where they were first bred. That's the Shetland Isles, the furthest-north part of Scotland.

They were working ponies, pulling carts, carrying peat and in the coal mines of Britain and, later, United States.

The Pony of the Americas, a popular riding breed in the U.S., is bred from Shetland Pony ancestors.

# Sea-faring ponies!

Sweet-natured, very strong and hard workers, Icelandic Ponies today are a popular breed among pony-loving kids!

How they got their name is even more interesting. It seems that when the Norsemen and Norsewomen sailed west, from their homes in what is now Norway, about 1,300 years ago, intending to settle and farm in Iceland, they took their cattle for food and their ponies for carrying heavy loads.

The cattle all died the first winter, due to the cold and harsh conditions. The tough little ponies, and some of the Norsepeople, survived.

*Settlers from Norway brought the first ponies to Iceland. These are feral Icelandic ponies.*

If you think you might like an Icelandic Pony, one thing about them you should know is that they walk with a rolling gait. To ride, you need to sit loose, letting your hips swing along with your pony's motion. Icelandic ponies are also a wide pony, requiring a broad saddle that is set back further on their backs than on other breeds of ponies or horses.

## Are ponies smart?

Like all animals, ponies developed to be exactly as smart as they need to be to find healthy food and clean drinking water, safe shelter, ways to protect

*Ponies always know how you're feeling. How do they do it?*

themselves from their enemies and have babies so their species would survive.

So, are they smarter than a dog? Or a monkey? Or a whale?

The answer is each of these has all the brainpower they need to thrive in the world they live in. They are each the smartest, in their own environment.

All types of horses, including ponies, have developed some pretty smart ways to thrive!

They use all their senses (that's taste, smell, touch, hearing and being able to see things) to find what they need.

Ponies have relationships with each other. They rely on their friends.

They can form close relationships with people they like and trust.

They have long memories. They remember a former owner, even if they haven't seen that person for many years.

But recently, experts have discovered that ponies can do even more than this. Modern scientists say that ponies are about as smart as the average child who is three years old.

Could it be they're even smarter than we think?

# Pony mind-readers?

Ponies, like all horses, can tell exactly what the other members of their herds are thinking.

But how do they do it? Is it mind-reading? Some kind of magic? Just luck?

No, none of these.

As prey animals, ponies are acutely aware of everything that's happening around them, always on-guard for the slightest hint of danger. All prey animals are herd animals because they need their herd-mates for protection.

Ponies and horses watch each other, and particularly what direction herd-mates' ears are pointing. If one pony startles and runs, the whole herd will. It's a question of skedaddle first, ask questions about why later.

# Ponies can recognize human feelings

Ponies are able to recognize human feelings and emotions. Not only that, they remember the angry person they met, or the sweet and kind person by what mood that person was in the last time they saw them!

It seems that in the thousands of years that horses and people have lived together and worked together, all types of horses including ponies have learned how to read people's faces and body language, as well as understand the tone of voice they use. The only other animal that can do this is dogs.

Horses are stressed when they see an angry face or hear angry voices. They like calm, quiet voices.

# Ponies can recognize themselves in a mirror

Many animals are afraid of or confused by what they see in a mirror or glass that reflects.

Not ponies! Like almost all horses, ponies are able to recognize themselves in a mirror. How do they know what they look like? Scientists and others who study animal behaviour have pondered this question but it's still a mystery

## Ponies will ask for help when they can't solve a problem

When ponies have problems they can't figure out, they will ask humans for help. In an experiment at Kobe University in Japan in 2016, horses knew that some delicious carrots were hidden where they couldn't reach them, but their caretakers didn't know this.

When the horses figured out that the humans were clueless about the carrots, they would first look at the place they were hidden. If their humans didn't get the hint, they'd touch and finally push their caregivers towards the carrot stash.

Not only did the horses figure out how to solve their problem (get carrots), they understood how to keep telling the humans until the humans got the message and delivered the carrot treats!

## Things ponies <u>really</u> don't like

Just like people, ponies are individuals. They each have their own distinct personality. But there are some things all ponies <u>really</u> don't like. If you do any of these things with your pony, they are going to be

*This is a piebald pony with rare blue eyes. Piebald means their coat is a mix of black and white patches.*

doing some serious tail swishing! And if you really annoy them and just don't listen to what they're trying to tell you – watch out!

Here's what ponies just hate:

1. **Loud voices** or people shouting. They like quiet, calm voices.
2. **Tack that doesn't fit**. Tack is all the things you use to ride a pony, such as the saddle, halter and bridle. Loose or bad tack can cause them to be sore or injured.
3. **Shoes that don't fit**. It hurts them to walk and can injure them.
4. **Poor riders**. They don't like having people on their backs who are sloppy or just don't know

what they're doing. (You probably wouldn't like that, either!)

5. **People who don't understand Pony Talk.** That's the sounds they make and also the body language of their ears, tail, legs, eyes and mouth.

6. **Being left in their stall too much**. They get bored. Unless they're sick, they'd always rather be running around outside with their herd.

7. **Having no horse friends**. As a herd animal, they feel happy, comforted and protected by their herd and nervous, lonely and scared with no mates. To a pony, a herd-mate can be a horse, donkey, pony or even a goat.

8. **People that are impatient or unkind**. Just like people, they learn best when they are treated with patience and kindness.

# Pony gaits

Gait is the word for how a pony moves his or her body. Ponies have four gaits. They are:

**Walk** – Ponies walk at about 4 miles per hour, or almost 6 ½ kilometres per hour.

**Trot** – A bit faster than walking. This is when they're making the clip-clop sound with their hooves.

**Canter** – A canter is a three-beat run, useful for going longer distances.

**Gallop** – In a burst of energy, a pony can gallop 25 to 30 miles per hour with a rider, or 32 to 48 kilometres per hour. Galloping gets a pony somewhere else quickly. They can only do it for two miles (just a bit more than 3 kilometres) before they are tired and need to walk instead.

# Strange sleepers!

Ponies only sleep for about a total of three hours every day. That's much less than most other mammals. Or people!

They don't do all their sleeping at one time. If you see a pony standing with their head down, ears relaxed, and one back leg bent, they are resting. They could even be taking a short nap! That's because they're able to lock their legs and sleep standing up.

Ponies like to take several short naps every day. They sleep standing up because it means if there is danger, they can wake up quickly and maybe run away.

But, like all mammals, including people, they also need some deep sleep every day (or night). To get this, they lie down and stretch out. They usually prefer to do this in their safe, comfortable stall in their stable.

On a warm summer day, several ponies in a herd may decide to have a little sleep in the sunshine, while a few members of the herd stay awake to stand guard.

Young ponies and seniors sleep more than adults do.

### *Pony Fun Fact:*
*Pony foals have a belly button.*

*2 boys riding their ponies.*

## How to tell if your pony is happy

The fast way to tell how your pony is feeling is to look at their ears.

Are their ears alert and pointing forward? It means they think they might have heard something in that direction. Now they have to decide whether to run.

Are they moving their ears back and forth rapidly? This means they're scared or maybe anxious about something. They're trying to figure out where the worrying sound is coming from.

Ears that are turned out to the side and sort of flopped over are the sign of a relaxed pony who is resting or sleeping. They feel safe and content.

If you notice your pony's ears are pined back and they are almost touching his or her neck, watch out! This means they're angry or feeling threatened. It's like you saying, "I don't like that. Stop it right now!"

# You know your pony is angry when...

Their face looks tense or angry. Ponies, like people, make and understand expressions on faces such as happy, sad, angry, worried or excited. If there are wrinkles around their eyes or muzzle, they are angry or in pain.

They are baring their teeth, rolling their eyes and their ears are laid back against their head. This shows they are seriously annoyed and thinking about biting someone.

They are stamping their hooves or pawing the ground. If they're pawing, they're probably bored and tired of being tied up, in their stall too long with nothing to do or ignored by you.

They're swishing their tail. Out in the field, they do this to chase flies away. This can also mean they're excited about something. They can also swish their tail when you're riding and they're not comfortable with something. It could be their tack just isn't fitting properly. Furious swishing means they are frustrated, feeling stress, or just plain angry.

They turn their backside to you. It means they might kick you next. The place you always want to be if you're near a horse or pony is their front end.

*Pony friends, feeling safe in their paddock.*

They look tense and lift a hind leg. This is different than their resting position of standing on three legs. Combined with the other signs, it means he or she is upset about something.

They have tight, pursed lips. In people, this sign means frustration or anger. That's also true for ponies. If their mouth looks tight, they are about to bite.

They're showing the whites of their eyes. This can also mean they are feeling stressed or afraid.

## Pony get-togethers

Where would you go if you want to know even more about ponies? Maybe even ride in pony competitions?

This would be a place where everyone you'd meet would love ponies as much as you do!

Unless you live in the centre of a big city, chances are there's a place like this, not too far from you right now. It will be called Pony Club Playdays, or perhaps Gymkhana. If you are in some parts of Western United States, it's known as O-mok-see or Omoksee.

These are all events for speed racing, jumping and riding for riders and their horses or ponies, including beginners and kids. It's a place to meet new friends and show off your pony as well as your riding skills, and maybe win a prize!

Even if you don't join in, it's a great place to see some fancy riding!

To find out where there are pony get-togethers near you, do an online search on Pony Club or 4-H Club + where you live. Many of these organizations also offer riding lessons.

If you live in or near a small town, there may also be county fairs where there are pony events.

# Pony passports

A passport is what identifies you when you travel to other countries. You have to show it to border guards to be allowed to go into other countries and also when you come home to your own country to prove who you are.

Some animals, in some places, also have passports. In all the EU countries in Europe, ponies need to have their own passports to go to pony events in other countries.

*Some foals can walk and run just an hour after they're born. Almost all foals can run by two hours after they're born.*

In UK (that's England, Wales, Scotland and Northern Ireland) ALL ponies must have their own passport by law, even if that pony never travels any further than his or her own field!

**Pony Fun Fact:**

*All ponies have four gaits, or ways of walking.*
*Icelandic ponies have six gaits.*

# There's no such thing as a Pony Whisperer

Perhaps you've heard about people who claim to be able to 'whisper' with their horse or pony, learning all his or her secrets. You may have met such a person, or could even come to see yourself holding this special skill as a Pony Whisperer.

After all, there are books and movies about people having such a mystical and magical skill. So why couldn't that be you, too?

Attractive as that idea might be, the truth is that there are people with empathy for others, including animals. They take the time and make the effort to truly walk in someone else's footsteps – or their hoof-prints. They CARE enough to try to understand behaviour, even if it isn't the way they'd act in the same situation.

The key here isn't the magic, it's the caring. Or possibly the caring IS the magic.

If you are one of these caring people, now that you've read this book, you know many more of ponies' closest-held secrets. If you are fortunate enough to have a pony in your life, now you know a lot more about who they are, what they like and what they really <u>don't</u> like.

You can understand that even the sweetest, most gentle and patient pony will get annoyed with bad behaviour from those around them, including the people in their lives. And when that happens, just like you or me or anyone, they're going to act up. A misunderstood pony is likely to be a mis-treated pony. And when that happens, prepare for a pony that kicks, bites, is stubborn and just plain unpleasant.

Once you know this, and you've learnt to listen to your pony and observe them as they tell you everything through their body language, you don't need any of that whispering nonsense. You will have become a responsible, caring pony owner, a better world citizen, and a happier person in the process.

Here's wishing you a long and joyous friendship with the sweet, gentle, intelligent and amazing pony in your life today, or in your future!

Fondly,

*Jacquelyn*

### Pony Fun Fact:
*Ponies didn't evolve. Humans bred them from different breeds of horses.*

### Pony Fun Fact:
*There are about 60 million horses and ponies in the world today.*

# About the Author

Jacquelyn Elnor Johnson started telling stories to entertain her younger sisters, discovering in the telling what it takes to engage your audience! By age 15, she was a correspondent for the local newspaper and had written her first book. She went on to have careers in writing for and editing newspapers and magazines and teaching journalism.

In 2014, she moved with her family to Nova Scotia, drawn by the opportunity to live near the ocean. With the move came a change to bring her writing full circle, returning to creating fun books for kids ages 6 to 12. A life-long pet lover, she is the bestselling author of 12 books about caring for and enjoying pets and animals, including I Want A Bearded Dragon and Fun Bearded Dragon & Leopard Gecko Facts.

In addition to writing practical, helpful and entertaining non-fiction, she writes novels including the Morley Stories series for girls ages 10 to 13.

Find all these books and more at
**www.CrimsonHillBooks.com**

# PHOTO CREDITS

Thank you to these photo artists:

Shutterstock:  James Hine, Julia Remezova, Paul Steven, Alla-B, Stefano Bolgnini, Julia Siomuha, Gorillaimages, Nika Z, Rita Kochmarjova, Groome, Pirita, Jill Richardson King and graphic artist Darko M.

Pixabay: Hans Braxmeier, Ute Becker, JackieLou DL, Waltteri Paulaharju, Uki 71, Elke Klostermann, Ainslie Gilles-Patel, David Mark, Cristel Sagniez, David Mark, Dewdrop 157, 165106, Pen Ash, Dariusz Labuda, Manfred Richter, Vevercolog, Viviane Monconduit, Photosforyou, Alexas Fotos, Anrita1705 and Paul Vom Ehrenberg.

# Loved all these great pony facts? Discover MORE Fun Facts books from Crimson Hill Books:

- **Fun Dog Facts for Kids**
- **Fun Cat Facts for Kids**
- **Fun Leopard Gecko and Bearded Dragon Facts for Kids**
- **Fun Reptile Facts for Kids; Lizards, Turtles, Crocodilians, Snakes and Birds**
- **Fun Pony Facts for Kids**
- **Fun Horse Facts for Kids**
- **Fun Bird Facts for Kids**
- **Fun Backyard Bird Facts for Kids**
- **Fun Insect Facts for Kids**

## And Don't Miss:

- **Dinosaur Facts for Kids**
- **T-rex Facts for Kids**